Introduction

Being a great athlete did not come easy to Tom Seaver. In high school he was too small to throw a fast ball. But Tom was determined to do his best. His hard work paid off. Today he is one of the finest pitchers in the history of baseball.

Tom Seaver

Marshall and Sue Burchard

Illustrated with photographs
and with drawings by Paul Frame

Harcourt Brace Jovanovich
New York and London

Library of Congress Cataloging in Publication Data

Burchard, Marshall.
　　Sports star: Tom Seaver.

　　SUMMARY: A brief biography of pitcher Tom Seaver,
who was instrumental in reversing the New York Mets
losing streak and helping them become the National
League champions.
　　1.　Seaver, Tom, 1944-　　—Juvenile literature.
2.　Baseball—Juvenile literature. [1. Seaver, Tom.
1944-　　2.　Baseball—Biography] I.　Burchard, Sue,
joint author.　II.　Title.
GV865.S4B87　　　796.357'092'4 [B] [92]　　74-7265
ISBN 0-15-277996-5
ISBN 0-15-278011-4

Contents

1

The Perfect Game

This is Tom Seaver. He is one of the finest pitchers in baseball. He pitches for the New York Mets.

Tom grew up in the town of Fresno, California. Tom's best friend, Russ, lived across the street. When Tom was six years old, he was not allowed to cross the street by himself. Russ was not allowed to cross the street either. "How can we play together?" Russ shouted to Tom. "We could play catch," Tom said. So they did.

The boys spent many hours throwing a ball back and forth across the street. They became good throwers and catchers. They did not

dare miss because they did not want to lose their ball in the street.

When Tom was eight years old, he tried out for the Little League. He did not make the team. When he got home, he went into his room. He cried and cried. His mother tried to make him feel better. She read him a story. It was called *The Little Engine That Could.* It was about a little train that had to pull a heavy load up a steep hill. The little engine told itself over and over, "I think I can. I think I can. I think I can."

The next year he made the Little League team. By the time Tom was eleven years old, he was the team's best hitter. He hit ten home runs that year. But a year later he found that what he did best was pitch. In one game he did a fantastic thing. He did not let one single batter get on base. When he was twelve years old, Tom Seaver pitched a perfect game!

2

Too Small to Be a Major Leaguer

Tom's whole family was athletic. His father played football and basketball in college. But what Mr. Seaver did best was play golf. For a time he was one of the finest amateur golfers in the country. Tom's mother liked to play golf, too. Mr. Seaver encouraged Tom's older brother and two sisters also to compete in sports. He was especially proud that at twelve years old Tom was a fine athlete.

But Mr. Seaver never pushed Tom into becoming a ballplayer. There were more important lessons he wanted Tom to learn. "You have to be willing to work hard," he told Tom. "You should try to be as perfect as possible in everything you do, even your household chores."

When Tom went to Fresno High School, he tried out for the varsity baseball team. The coaches looked him over. Then they told him he was too small to be on the team. Tom

was very disappointed and discouraged. But he did not give up. He worked at becoming a better pitcher. Since he was not big enough to throw the ball fast and hard, he tried throwing the ball at different speeds. He learned how to throw all kinds of crazy curves. He began to fool batters with his tricky pitches.

But no matter how hard Tom worked, there was not much he could do to make his body grow

faster. By his third year in high school he was still little and skinny. He was not yet strong enough or fast enough to make the varsity team. He began to give up his dream of becoming a major leaguer.

In the spring of his last year at

Fresno High, Tom tried out for the varsity baseball team again. This time he made it. He was the team's starting pitcher.

The year was 1962. It was the same year that a new big league team called the New York Mets played their first game. Tom did not know much about the Mets. He knew only that they lost most of the time. Tom's favorite team was the Los Angeles Dodgers.

Tom did his best, but he was not a great high school pitcher. He won six games and lost five. It was not a very exciting record. Tom's arm was still not strong enough to throw a good fast ball.

After the season was over, scouts from the big leagues talked to some of Tom's teammates. A few of his friends were offered the chance to play pro ball. But no scout came around to talk to Tom.

When he got out of high school, Tom did not know what he wanted to do. He tried to forget that he ever wanted to play in the big leagues.

3

Joining the Marines

For a while Tom worked for the same company as his father. The company sold fruit to food stores.

It was not easy work. Tom had to leave home at five-thirty every morning. His job was to unpack heavy boxes of raisins that came in from the fields. Sometimes Tom found snakes coiled in the bottom of the boxes. Other times rats jumped out. Tom did not like lifting the big boxes. He was afraid of the snakes and the rats.

After six months he quit and joined the Marines. The Marine officers were very strict. One time Tom forgot to clean his rifle. "You will have to be punished for this, Seaver," shouted a sergeant. The sergeant made Tom lift the heavy rifle up and down over his head for three hours. Tom thought he would die, he got so tired. At the end of the three hours he ached all over. He could not even lift his arms.

The new Marines were not al-

lowed to talk during meals. One day
Tom had a piece of blueberry pie he
did not want. "Do you want my pie?"
Tom whispered softly to a friend.

An officer at the other end of the table heard Tom. The officer got so angry that he jumped up on the table and marched over the dishes to where Tom sat. "Seaver!" he yelled. "Was that you?" Tom did not answer. That made the officer even angrier. He kicked Tom in the side. Food went flying in all directions.

He was glad to finish his active Marine duty six months later. When he left, Tom had changed. He was bigger and stronger and a lot more grown up. But he still did not know what he wanted to do next.

4

Going to College

Tom was sure of one thing. He did not want to go back to lifting raisin boxes.

In the fall of 1963, Tom entered Fresno City College. He tried out for the baseball team there.

At an early practice he made a wonderful discovery. Lifting the heavy raisin boxes and training in the Marines had been good for him.

He was finally strong enough to throw a blazing fast ball.

With his new strength, there was almost no stopping Tom. He won eleven games and lost two. At the end of the season he won eight games in a row. He was voted the Most Valuable Player on the Fresno City College team.

On the last day of school Tom was happy and feeling playful. He got in his car and went for a drive. A pretty girl was walking down the street. Her name was Nancy Lynn McIntyre. She had been in Tom's English class, but he had never

really met her. Tom slammed on the
brakes and jumped out of the car.
He ran over to Nancy and tackled
her. Before she could say a word, he
picked her up and put her in his car.

"Do you want to go to a softball game?" Tom asked her.

"No!" said Nancy. Tom laughed and took her anyway. Nancy had a good time. It was an odd way to meet a girl. But it worked. Tom and Nancy soon became good friends.

5

Tom Becomes a Met

The next year Tom got a scholarship to go to a bigger school. It was called the University of Southern California, or USC for short.

Tom still did not quite believe he could make a living as a baseball player, so he decided to study to become a dentist. Then he and Nancy could get married. But he kept playing baseball. A friend told Tom lifting weights would make him even stronger. He started working out with small weights every day.

By the end of the year Tom could throw an exploding fast ball. One day the USC team played a practice game against the Dodgers. Tom pitched. To his surprise he found he could strike out major league hitters. Three years earlier he had been having trouble striking out high school hitters!

He was so good that the Los Angeles Dodgers made him an offer to play pro ball. Tom turned down the offer.

He asked for more money. "We can't pay your price," said the Dodgers. "Good-by and good luck. We hope you become a fine dentist."

Tom stayed in college, but he still kept on playing baseball.

Baseball became more and more important to him. He decided he would rather be a big league ballplayer than anything else.

In his third year at USC Tom got a good offer from the Milwaukee Braves. He signed the contract and got ready to leave school. But when the Commissioner of Baseball heard about it, he was angry. He said Tom was not allowed to sign a pro contract while he was going to school. Tom tore up the contract and went back to his studies again.

After a year at USC, three big league teams wanted him. They were the Cleveland Indians, the Philadelphia Phillies, and the New York Mets. And they were all willing to pay him a lot of money.

Tom was not allowed to choose the team he wanted. Officials from the three ball clubs had a meeting to decide who would get him. They each wrote the name of their team on a piece of paper. They put the papers in a hat and shook them around and around. One man drew a slip of paper out of the hat and reached for the telephone. Tom's mother answered the phone.

"I have now drawn the name out of the hat," the man said. "And the name is"—he paused—"the NEW YORK METS!"

Tom discusses being a Met with his father.

6

Rookie of the Year

Tom was glad he was playing for the Mets. He knew they really needed a good young pitcher.

The Mets had finished in last place for four years in a row. They were the worst team in the major leagues. Their manager, Casey Stengel, called them the "Amazin' Mets" because they found so many ways to lose a game. The team was the biggest joke in baseball. But

Tom was determined to change all that. Two days after Tom signed his contract, he flew to the Mets' minor league training camp in Florida. He had to prove himself as a minor league player before he could become a big leaguer.

It didn't take long. Tom won his first pro game by a score of 4 to 2. He not only pitched well, but he also drove in two runs by hitting a double. As he slid into second base, lights on the scoreboard flashed the words "SUPER ROOKIE." Tom's teammates nicknamed him "Supe." The name stuck.

Pitching against the Pittsburgh Pirates.

Tom was happy, but he was lonely too. He called Nancy and asked her to come to Florida and marry him. Nancy said yes!

The next season, 1967, Tom was in the Mets' starting line-up. He pitched his first big league game against the Pittsburgh Pirates. The Mets won by a score of 3 to 2.

Some people cracked jokes after the game. "Well, the Amazing Mets finally won one," they said, laughing. "From now on they will go downhill." Tom did not think the joke was funny. He was not used to losing.

The Mets' pitching coach, Rube Walker, showed Tom how to make his fast ball suddenly change direction just as it reached a hitter. He practiced until he could do it perfectly.

Tom took his job very seriously. He started keeping a written record on every hitter. He made notes on each batter's strengths and weaknesses. When Tom faced a man at the plate, he knew what kind of pitch might get him out.

The hard work paid off. In his first season with the Mets, Tom proved he was the best pitcher on

Tom is congratulated by his teammates
after the All-Star Game in 1967.

the team. He won sixteen games. He struck out 170 men. He was named Rookie of the Year.

Despite Tom's good pitching the Mets still lost most of their games. Once more they finished in last place. In 1968, the Mets got a new manager, Gil Hodges. They began to win more often. Jerry Koosman, Nolan Ryan, and Tug McGraw helped Tom with the pitching. Outfielders Cleon Jones and Tommie Agee belted out a lot of hits. The Mets won almost half of their games. It was their best year so far.

Once again Tom won sixteen
games. He had 205 strikeouts.
Tom's teammates admired his deter-
mination to be the best. He became
the team's leader.

7

National League Champions

Most baseball fans thought the Mets would always be a last-place team. But by the 1969 season Tom and his teammates began to feel differently. They believed 1969 could be a good year for them.

Tom pitched their opening game against the Montreal Expos. But the whole team played so poorly that they lost. People kept right on laughing at the "Amazing Mets." Then, as if by magic, the Mets suddenly began winning most of their games.

When Tom was twelve years old, he had pitched his first and only perfect game. He had not allowed a single hit. Now, thirteen years later, on a hot night in Chicago, he had another perfect game going. The game was in the ninth inning. All he had to do was get three more batters out. Tom had no trouble getting out the Cubs' first batter. Then a batter named Jimmy Quails came to the plate. Tom threw a sinker, but it didn't sink. Quails swung and hit the ball to left center field. Two of the fastest Mets, Jones and Agee, raced to catch the ball. But they were too late. The ball fell for a single.

Tom's perfect game was ruined. He felt numb. He stood and stared into center field. "Don't let down," outfielder Donn Clendenon yelled. "Let's get the last two outs." Tom did and won the game by a score of 4 to 0, but he walked off the field a very disappointed man. A perfect game had been so close. "It was right there within my reach. Will I

have another chance?" he won-
dered.

The Mets kept up their winning

Tom shows his disappointment at
missing out on a perfect game.

streak. By August 15 they were nine and a half games behind the first-place Chicago Cubs. A month later they were three and a half games ahead of the Cubs and in first place. On September 24 the Mets clinched the Eastern Division title of the National League. Everybody on the Mets played his best all season long. Manager Gil Hodges made all the right moves. Agee and Jones had a terrific year at bat. The pitching staff was first-rate.

And Tom had his most brilliant season. In the final rush for the pennant, he was unbeatable. He won every game he pitched after August 5. He finished the season winning twenty-five games and losing only seven. He had 208 strikeouts. He won the Cy Young Award as the National League's most outstanding pitcher.

The Mets didn't stop with winning the Eastern Division title. They clobbered the Western Division winner, the Atlanta Braves, in three straight games.

The Mets were National League Champions! When they went to Baltimore for the World Series, they were determined to win.

8

The Amazing Mets

The Mets faced the Baltimore Orioles in the World Series. The first team to win four games would be world champions.

The Mets had never played in a World Series. Most baseball fans thought New York didn't stand a chance against the powerful Baltimore team.

The people of New York City were

Starting pitchers Mike Cuellar of the Orioles and Tom Seaver of the Mets.

excited. They had not had a winning baseball team for a long time. The whole city was rooting for the spunky young team that had been the laughing stock of baseball. Tom pitched in the first game of the Series. Baltimore won. Tom felt bad, but he knew he would have a chance to do better. The Mets won the next two games.

The fourth game was played in New York at Shea Stadium. It was an important game. If Baltimore won, the series would be tied two to two. But if New York won, the Mets would go ahead three games to one.

They would need only one more victory to win the Series.

Tom was pitching. He walked out to the mound and looked around. There was not a single empty seat. He saw the box where his whole family was sitting. He saw the big TV cameras aimed straight at him. "This is my chance to show the world that the Mets are winners," said Tom to himself. But he was nervous. He gave himself a pep talk. "Come on, Tom," he said. "You're the best pitcher in baseball. Just pitch the way you know how and you'll win. You can do it."

Seaver pitching to Oriole Don Buford.

After striking out the first Baltimore batter, Tom stopped feeling so nervous. His pitches were working. His fast ball was moving. The ball went just where he wanted it to go. "I think I can. I think I can," he said to himself.

In the second inning Donn Clendenon smashed a home run for the Mets. The Mets led by a score of 1 to 0. Tom was pitching well, but so was the star Baltimore pitcher, Mike Cuellar. The game turned into a battle between two of the greatest pitchers in baseball. Neither team was able to score any more runs.

Tom winding up for a fast ball.

When Tom walked out to the mound in the ninth inning, he had one thing on his mind. "Just three more outs," he thought. "And the game is ours. I'm a little tired, but I think I can do it."

Tom struck out the first batter. Then the Orioles got men on first and third base. Brooks Robinson came to bat and hit a hard liner into center field. Ron Swoboda made a flying dive for the ball. It was a fantastic catch. But one run scored. The game was tied 1 to 1. Tom was discouraged, but he struck out the next batter for the third out.

New York City honors the Mets with a ticker-tape parade.

The Seavers—Tom, Sarah, and Nancy—are a happy family after the World Series win.

The game went into extra innings. The Mets scored a run in the tenth inning and won the game.

Now there was nothing that could stop them. They beat Baltimore again in the next game. After losing the opening game of the Series, the Mets had gone on to win four straight. They were World Champions.

A reporter asked ex-manager Casey Stengel what he thought of the Mets' victory. "Amazin'," he said. All of New York City was in love with the Amazing Mets.

9

Trying to Be the Best

Tom has worked hard to become the fine athlete he is today. Pitching has never been easy for him. He spends almost all of his time keeping in shape and practicing.

"Pitching is what makes me happy," he says. "It tells me what to eat. It tells me when I have to go to bed. It tells me what to do when I am awake."

To keep his body strong, Tom still lifts weights every day. He runs to keep his legs in shape.

He has to make sure that he does not gain too much weight. When Tom feels like having a cookie, he has to tell himself, "No." He has to eat cottage cheese instead.

Tom has to pay special attention to his valuable pitching hand. He has to remember never to pet strange dogs or put a log on the fire with his right hand. But to Tom the hard work and care of his body has been worth it.

In 1973 Tom's strong pitching

helped put the Mets in the thick of another pennant race. In August the Mets went into a bad slump. Manager Yogi Berra read a newspaper article to his team. "Look," he said, pointing to the paper. "You are terrible. It says so right here. It says you guys don't want to play any more." After that the Mets got hot. Tom won ball game after ball game.

It was a close pennant race. For a while it looked as though there might be a five-way tie between the Mets, the Pirates, the Cardinals, the Expos, and the Cubs. But the Mets pulled ahead in September. In early October Tom pitched the winning game for the Mets. Once again they were the champions of the Eastern Division of the National League.

The Amazing Mets went on to do what most fans thought was impossible. They defeated the powerful Western Division champions, the Cincinnati Reds, to become the National League Champions.

Then they faced the Oakland Athletics in the World Series. Tom's arm was getting tired. He had pitched too often in the last few weeks. Some of the other Met

Tom Seaver, manager Yogi Berra, and pitcher Tug McGraw
celebrate winning the National League East title.